CAT AND DOG
JOKES

Katy Hall & Lisa Eisenberg

Illustrated by H.L. Schwadron

SCHOLASTIC INC.
New York Toronto London Auckland Sydney

ISBN 0-590-43336-9

21 20 19 18 17   8 9/9 0/0

Printed in the U.S.A.   01

First Scholastic printing, April 1990

*To Leighsh McMullan and Kat,
Annie-gora, and Tomutt Eisenberg*

KITTY CAPURRS

Have you heard the joke about the cat on the roof?

Never mind. It's over your head!

Why did the cat want to become a nurse?

She wanted to be a first-aid kit!

When is it unlucky to have a black
cat cross your path?

When you're a mouse!

What kind of cat has eight legs?

An octo-puss!

What do people in England call
little black cats?

Kittens!

FIDO, SPEAK!

What did the dog say to the flea?

"Don't bug me!"

In what month do dogs bark the least?

February — it's the shortest month!

What should you do if your dog starts to chew up your dictionary?

Take the words right out of his mouth!

What do you get if you cross a
black hunting dog with a
telephone?

A labrador receiver!

7

KNOCK, KNOCK!

Knock, knock!
Who's there?
Pooch!
Pooch who?
Pooch your arms around me, baby!

Knock, knock!
Who's there?
Purr!
Purr who?
Purr-sonally, I'd prefer to keep my
    distance!

Knock, knock!
Who's there?
Oliver!
Oliver who?
Oliver sudden my dog went crazy!

Knock, knock!
Who's there?
Hans!
Hans who?
Hans off my cat!

CAT AND DOG
TV GUIDE

9:00 A.M.	Cartoon: Pupeye the Sailor
10:00 A.M.	Movie: The Ka-*ratty* Kit
11:00 A.M.	Cartoon: The Ghostbowsers
12:00 P.M.	Talk show: Sally Jessy *Ruff*ael
1:00 P.M.	Soap opera: Nine Lives To Live
2:00 P.M.	Talk show: *Grrrrr*aldo Rivera
3:00 P.M.	Situation Comewdy: Kate and Alpo
4:00 P.M.	Jeo*purr*dy!
5:00 P.M.	The Price Is Right, starring Bob *Bark*er
6:00 P.M.	Heavyweight Boxering in History with Muhammad Alleycat

CRAZY CROSSES!

What would you get if you crossed a
puppy with a mean boy?

A bully dog!

What would you get if you crossed a
chili pepper, a steam shovel, and a
chihuahua?

A hot diggity dog!

What would you get if you crossed a
cat and a donkey?

A mewl.

What would you get if you crossed a
pit bull and a cow?

An animal that's too mean to milk!

What would you get if you crossed a
cat and a pair of galoshes?

Puss 'n' boots!

What would you get if you crossed a
dog and a cat?

An animal that chases itself!

DOG GONE!

What barks, chases cats, and has black and red spots?

A dalmation with the measles!

Which dogs bark more, old ones or young ones?

It's about arf and arf!

What do dogs always take on their camping trips?

Pup tents!

Kate: Did you like the story about the dog who ran two miles just to pick up a stick?

Nate: No, I thought it was a little farfetched!

LEADERS ON LEASHES

What dogs became President of the
United States?

Rover Cleveland.
Zachary Tailer.
Rufferford Hayes.
Chester A. Arfer.
Dwight D. Eisenhowler.
George Bushy-tail.
William McKinleash.

CAT-ASTROPHE!

What do kittens like to put on their burgers?

Catsup!

What's another name for a cat burglar?

A purr-snatcher!

What kind of cats like to go bowling?

Alley cats!

What Broadway show do cats like?

The Sound of Mewsic!

What song do cats adore?

"Felines . . . nothing left but felines. . . ."

What award can a dramatic feline hope to win?

An A-cat-emy Award!

Father: How do you get Sonny up in the mornings?
Mother: I just throw the cat on his bed.
Father: How does that get him up?
Mother: Sonny sleeps with the dog!

DATS AND COGS

What do you get if you cross a mutt and a poodle?

A muddle.

How do you spell *mousetrap* in three letters?

C–A–T!

What did the puppy say to the shoe?

It's been nice gnawing you!

JOLLY COLLIES

What do you call a mutt's coat?

Cur fur!

What do you call a dog's kiss?

A pooch smooch!

What do you call a chubby dog?

A round hound!

What do you call a meeting among many dogs?

A bow-wow pow-wow!

What do you call a dog's spaghetti?

Poodle's noodles!

What do you call a happier hunting dog?

A merrier terrier!

Meg: Do you know how to keep a pit bull from charging?

Peg: Yes.... Take away its credit cards.

DANGEROUS DOGGIES!

What do you get if you cross a
watchdog and a vampire?

A pale mailman!

What happened to the dog that ate
only garlic and onions?

His bark was worse than his bite!

KNOCK, KNOCK AGAIN!

Knock, knock!
Who's there?
Howl!
Howl who?
Howl we get away from that mean
   dog over there?

Knock, knock!
Who's there?
Puss!
Puss who?
Puss-ibly we could climb that tree!

Knock, knock!
Who's there?
Flea!
Flea who?
Flea from that dog before he bites
  us!

Knock, knock!
Who's there?
Claws!
Claws who?
Claws the door behind us!

BACKWARDS RIDDLES!

Answer: *Scare-de-cat.*
Question: Which one of your pets should you scare on Halloween?

Answer: *Doggone!*

Question: What do you say when you call your dog and he doesn't come?

BITING REMARKS!

Joe: Hey! Your dog took a bite out of my apple!

Flo: Big deal! I'll get you another apple!

Joe: But it was my Adam's apple!

June: Hey! Your dog just bit me on the ankle!

Goon: Well, he's too short to reach your knee!

Sue: I play chess with my dog every day.

Prue: Wow, your dog must be really smart!

Sue: Oh, not really. I usually beat him.

Cowboy: Say, why'd you buy that
there dachshund?
City Slicker: I heard someone say,
"Get a long, little doggy!"

CAT CALLS

What do you call what cats read to stay up-to-date?

The Daily Mews Purr-per.

What do you call the place where cats look up library books?

The card cat-alog.

What do you call a cat surrounded by a hundred mice?

Purr-fectly happy!

HOWLS AND YOWLS

What dog should you ask for the time of day?

A watchdog!

Why do dogs chase their tails?

They're trying to make both ends meet!

What was the first cat to fly?

Kitty-hawk!

What kind of dog has a bark but no bite?

A dogwood!

What do you call a lemon-eating cat?

A sour puss!

HOLLYWOOD HOT SHOTS

Meg: Look! There's Pawl Newman!

Peg: And isn't that Robert Waggin'er talking to Elizabeth Tailer?

Meg: Over there! I see Cur-rie Fisher!

Peg: Ooooh! And Mutt Dillon!

Meg: And here comes that one who does all the interviews!

Peg: You mean Bow-Wow Walters?

Meg: Right. You know, this party's really for the dogs!

WHAT'S THE DIF?

What's the difference between a cat and a frog?

A cat has nine lives, but a frog croaks every night!

What's the difference between a match and a cat?

A match lights on its head and a cat lights on its feet!

What's the difference between a baseball player and his tired dog?

The ballplayer wears a complete uniform, but the dog only pants!

CATS IN CHARGE!

How many cats have been elected
President of the United States?

Thomeows Jefferson.
Grow-fur Cleveland.
James Meowonroe.
Hairy S. Truman.
Jimmy Catter.
Dwight D. Eisenmeower.
And, of course, James A. Garfield!

Why is a cat in the Sahara like Christmas?

Because of its Sandy Claws!

KNOCK 'EM OUT!

Knock, knock!
Who's there?
Bow!
Bow who?
Not bow who, bow *wow*!

Knock, knock!
Who's there?
Ron!
Ron who?
Ron a little faster, will you? There's
a pit bull after us!

Knock, knock!
Who's there?
Neil!
Neil who?
Neil down and pet this cat!

Knock, knock!
Who's there?
Juan!
Juan who?
Juan day I'll get a cat of my own!

Knock, knock!
Who's there?
Doughnut.
Doughnut who?
Doughnut pull my dog's tail, or
he'll bite you!

Knock, knock!
Who's there?
Theodore!
Theodore who?
Theodore is stuck, and my dog can't
get out!

What do you call a dog with royal blood?

A regal beagle.

LUNCHING
AT THE CATATERIA

THE PAWS
THAT REFRESHES!

If there were ten cats in a boat and one jumped out, how many would be left?

None! They were all copycats!

What should you give your dog
when he does a good job?

A bone-us!

When is a cat most likely to run
out of the house?

When the door is open!

What did the dog say when it got
its tail caught in the door?

"It won't be long now!"

Funny: Did you hear about the dog that went to the flea circus?
Bunny: No, what happened?
Funny: He stole the show!

DIFFERENT STROKES

What's the difference between a dog from Nebraska and a flea?

One howls on the prairie and the other prowls on the hairy!

What's the difference between a cat and a comma?

One has claws at the end of its paws, and the other a pause at the end of its clause!

Where does a dog go when it loses
its tail?

To a re-tail shop.

Fred: Did you ever see a catfish?
Ed: No! How did she hold the rod and reel?

WEATHER OR NOT....

What's the worse weather for mice?

When it's raining cats and dogs!

What's even *worse* weather than raining cats and dogs?

Hailing taxicabs!

What dog must you be careful not to step on in a storm?

A poodle!

Donny: How do you like my police dog?

Bonny: I never saw a police dog that looked like *that* before!

Donny: Of course not! He's working undercover!

WITTY KITTIES

What do you call a chubby kitty?

A fat cat!

What do you call a cat who works out?

A fit kit!

What do you call a threadbare cat?

A shabby tabby!

What do you call an urban feline?

A city kitty!

What do you call a cross between a cat and a skunk?

A mew pew!

Nancy Lou: I'd like to buy a puppy.

Pet Store Owner: They're ten dollars apiece.

Nancy Lou: How much for a whole puppy?

DOG-EARED JOKES!

Moss: I can pick up a cent with my toes.

Ross: Big deal. My dog can do it with his nose!

Leigh: Say, is that dog a pointer?

Dee: No, it's a disappointer.

NOW HEAR HISS!

Did you hear about the cat who swallowed the ball of yarn?

She had mittens!

Did you hear about the cat who swallowed the duck?

She became a duck-filled fatty-puss!

Did you hear about the cat who ran up the big phone bill?

She called Persian-to-Persian!

WE'RE NOT HOME!

Knock, knock!
Who's there?
Catsup.
Catsup who?
Catsup a tree and she won't come
  down!

Knock, knock!
Who's there?
Terry.
Terry who?
Terry bull she can't get down!

Knock, knock!
Who's there?
Frank Lee.
Frank Lee who?
Frank Lee she can stay up there for
all I care!

Knock, knock!
Who's there?
Harry.
Harry who?
Harry up and bring me a ladder!

Teacher: What is a comet?

Annie: A star with a tail.

Teacher: Good. Can you name one?

Annie: Lassie!

66

Teacher: Name four members of the cat family.

Kate: The mother cat, the father cat, and two kittens!

PURR-FECTLY AWFUL!

What do you get if you cross a
kitten with a post?

A cat-er-pillar!

What do you call a kitten fight?

A cat-astrophe!

What are the last two hairs on a cat's tail called?

Cat hairs.

What do you get if you cross a kitten and a little girl's hairdo?

A braidy-cat!

THE UNITED STATES OF AMERICAT!

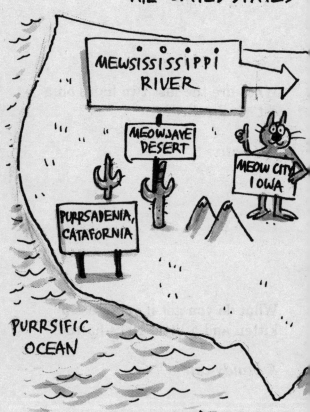

DOGGEREL!

Why are dogs like very affectionate children?

They lick their paws!

What's the best way to keep a dog from smelling?

Hold its nose!

What kind of dog can jump higher than a house?

Any kind! A house can't jump!

What would you get if you crossed a parrot and a pit bull?

Who knows? But when it talks, you'd better listen!

What did one flea say to the other when they came out of the movie?

"Shall we walk home or take the greyhound?"

What did the dog's right eye say to his left eye?

"Just between us, something smells!"

Dad: Why is Fido sitting outside in the sun like that?

Tommy: You told me to have a hot dog for lunch!

GO AWAY!

Knock, knock!
Who's there?
Sarah!
Sarah who?
Sarah dog in there with you?

Knock, knock!
Who's there?
Ken!
Ken who?
Ken I bring my dog inside?

Knock, knock!
Who's there?
Arthur!
Arthur who?
Arthur any more dogs out there?

Knock, knock!
Who's there?
Isabel!
Isabel who?
Isabel really necessary on this
    collar?

FLICKS OF THE TAIL!

DOG LAND, U.S.A.

U.S.A.

Jim's dog, Fido, came home from school with a terrible report card.

"But my foreign-language teacher says I'm improving," Fido assured Jim.

"Okay," said Jim. "Say something in a foreign language."

"Meow!" said the dog.

TEACHER'S PET
READING LIST

Cat the Bunny
Hairyette the Spy
James and the Giant Pooch
Mrs. Frisby and the Cats of NIMH
The Phan-tom-cat Tollbooth
Rameowna the Pest
Winnie the Pooch
War and Puss

DOGGIE BONERS!

What do you get if you cross a beagle and bread dough?

Dog biscuits!

And what is the main ingredient of dog biscuits?

Collie-flour!

What kind of dog can fly?

A bird dog!

Why does a dog turn around three times before lying down?

Because "one good turn deserves another"!

Why did the policeman give the dog a ticket?

He was in a NO BARKING zone!

CAT AND DOG MEW-SIC GROUPS AND SINGERS!

The Beagles
Bone Jovi
The Rolling Bones
(M)U–2
Phil Colliens
El Debark
Duran Duranafterthemouse

HARDBARK
AND PAPURRBACK
BEST-SELLERS!

Housebreaking Your Dog
by Hope N. Deedore

Housebreaking Your Cat
by Phil D. Littreboxx

Can Cats and Dogs Be Friends?
by Dawn B. Leevit

Will Your Cat Eat Your Hamster?
by Betty Will

Brushing Your Doberman's Teeth
by Hugo First

The Hound That Howled All Night
by Major Headache

Breaking Up a Cat and Dog Fight
by Luke Out

Escaping from Your Pets
by Clem A. Tree and Ron N. Hyde

CROSS-EYED CROSSES!

What would you get if you crossed a kitten with a melon?

A cat-aloupe!

What would you get if you crossed a kitten and a mackerel?

A catfish!

What would you get if you crossed a cat and an octagon?

An octo-puss!

What would you get if you crossed a sheepdog and a kangaroo?

A fur coat with pockets!

What would you get if you crossed a two-toned cat and an exhaust pipe?

A skunk!

What kind of transportation do dogs like?

Greyhound!

ROVER'S RIDDLES

Why is the nose in the middle of a
bloodhound's face?

Because it's the scenter!

Why did the dog jump into the
river?

He wanted to chase the catfish!

Why does a dog wag its tail?

Because no one will wag it for him!

EVEN CRAZIER CROSSES!

What do you get if you cross a camera with a pit bull?

A snapshot!

What do you get if you cross a beagle with a giraffe?

A dog that barks at airplanes!

What do you get if you cross a cat
with a canary?

A happy cat!

CAT'S ALL, FOLKS!

What has fur and whiskers and cuts grass?

A lawn meower!

Why is a cat longer at night than in the morning?

Because you let a cat out at night and take him in in the morning!

Why are cats like bad surgeons?

Because they mew-till-late and destroy patience!

How many cats were born in Nebraska last year?

None! Only kittens were born!

What did the cat say when she burned her tail?

"This is the end of me!"